Sing tha

Sing that joke

Paul Cookson

solway

Dedicated to
Ian M and David H
Thanks

Copyright © 1998 Paul Cookson

First published in 1998 by Solway

04 03 02 01 00 99 98   7 6 5 4 3 2 1

Solway is an imprint of Paternoster Publishing,
P.O. Box 300, Carlisle, Cumbria, CA3 0QS, U.K.
http://www.paternoster-publishing.com

The right of Paul Cookson to be identified as the Author of this Work has been
asserted by him in accordance with Copyright, Designs and Patents Act 1988.

*All rights reserved. No part of this publication may be reproduced,
stored in a retrieval system, or transmitted in any form or by any
means, electronic, mechanical, photocopying, recording or otherwise,
without the prior permission of the publisher or a licence permitting
restricted copying. In the U.K. such licences are issued by the
Copyright Licensing Agency,
90 Tottenham Court Road, London W1P 9HE.*

British Library Cataloguing in Publication Data
A catalogue record for this book is available from the British Library

ISBN 1-900507-79-X

Some of these poems first appeared in the following collections by Paul Cookson:
The Amazing Captain Concorde (1990), Happy as a Pig in Muck (1991), The Toilet Seat
Has Teeth! (1992), Rhyming Rhythms for Twisted Tongues (1993)

Cover design by David Parkins
Typeset by WestKey Ltd, Cornwall
Printed in Great Britain by
Caledonian International Book Manufacturing Ltd, Glasgow

Contents

Infants and assemblies: lining up, sitting down, shoes, dresses and trousers

Wibbly wobbly aliens
Wiggly lines
Thumb sucking
Head spinning
Backwards walking
Beam into assembly . . .

Some are facing left
Some are facing right
Some are lying down
Some are standing on their heads
Some are standing on other people's heads . . .

They always wear shoes with Velcro because
They can't tie their laces at all
So it's KRRRCH! KRRRCH! "Pass it on"
. . . A big pile of shoes at the end of the hall.

Little girls lift their dresses
Over their heads, high in the air . . .

Rows and rows and rows and rows
Of Care Bear Knickers everywhere.

One hand in their mouth
The other down their pants
Little boys slurp and twirl
Slurp twirl then swap hands!

The Amazing Captain Concorde

5 4 3 2 1 . . . BLAST OFF!
Is it a bird?
Is it a plane?
Look at the size of the nose on his face!
Is it a bird?
Is it a plane?
Captain Concorde is his name!
Captain Concorde NEEOWN!
What a big nose NEEOWN!

He's a man with a mission
Radar vision
A nose that's supersonic
Faster than the speed of sound
His y fronts are bionic
Big and baggy
Red and saggy
Streamlined underpants
Always ready
Hi tech shreddies
Crooks don't stand a chance . . .

IS IT A BIRD? etc.

Anytime anyplace anywhere
But never ever Mondays
Cos that's the day the Captain's mum
Washes his red undies.
Anytime anyplace anywhere
His power is fantastic
Everything's under control
With super strength elastic!
Anytime anywhere anyplace
But bathrooms are a no no
Cos the toilet seat has teeth! OW!
And then it's time to go so . . .

IS IT A BIRD? etc.

The Amazing Captain Concorde . . . he's a superman.
The Amazing Captain Concorde . . . super underpants.
The Amazing Captain Concorde . . . indestructable
The Amazing Captain Concorde . . . incorruptible

Who's the man with the supersonic nose? . . . Captain Concorde!
Who's the man with the terrible taste in clothes? . . . Captain Concorde!
Who's the man who's always your best friend? . . . Captain Concorde!
Who's the man who always sets the trends? . . . Captain Concorde

Who's the man who's so aerodynamic? . . . Captain Concorde!
Who's the man who makes all villains panic? . . . Captain Concorde!
Who's the man who always helps his mum? . . . Captain Concorde!
Who's the man you'd all like to become? . . . Captain Concorde!
Who? Captain Concorde!
Who? Captain Concorde!
Soooooo . . .

IS IT A BIRD? etc.

Frog in my throat

There's a frog in my throat
and it's making me croak
and I'm coughing so much I think I'll choke

It's raw . . . and sore
and I don't know what it's doing it for
that frog in my throat with a big chainsaw
that draws and saws
right across my vocal chords
like long and sharp serrated swords
splintered just like cheap floorboards
or rusty hinges on a door
and I don't think I can take any more

There's a frog in my throat
and it's making me croak
and I'm coughing so much I think I'll choke

There's a frog in my throat
thinks it's a joke
to get a sharp stick and start to poke

From side to side
up and down till my throat has dried
like a river bed cracked open wide
when all that's left is the dust inside
it's died, died
my throat is shrivelled, my tongue is tied
that frog is taking me for a ride

There's a frog in my throat
and it's making me croak
and I'm coughing so much I think I'll choke

There's a frog in my throat
thinks it's a joke
to get a sharp stick and start to poke

That frog in my throat
is wearing a coat
of holly, barbed wire and frayed steel rope

4

That vicious frog in my throat is rotten
jogging in clogs with spikes on the bottom
hopping and bopping and there's no stopping
all this cutting and garotting
like bayonets underneath a toboggan
the rotten frog just keeps on flogging
up and down my epiglottis
until all that I have got is
a red raw throat inflamed and frayed
vocal chords sliced and splayed
digging down my neck with a spade
with a hammer and chisel in the middle it's made
its mark with a drill and a razor blade
exploding like a hand grenade
every time I splutter and cough
a rattling gattling gun going off

There's a frog in my throat
and it's making me croak
and I'm coughing so much I think I'll choke

There's a frog in my throat
thinks it's a joke
to get a sharp stick and start to poke

That frog in my throat
is wearing a coat
of holly, barbed wire and bicycle spokes

That frog in my throat
is starting to gloat
and the chance of a cure is looking remote

It's bleak, I'm weak
look at the state of my physique
all you hear is a feeble squeak
every time I try to speak
it sounds like a rusty gate with a creak

That frog, it drops
lots and lots and lots and lots
wheelbarrow loads of rubble and rocks
chalk dust into my voicebox
that locks and blocks
my throat and ties my tongue in knots

I sneeze and wheeze
and I can hardly breathe
that frog in my throat begins to seize
my tonsils in an orange squeeze
so that every time I sneeze
it feels like a grater grating cheese
please, please
that frog has got me on my knees

Playing tennis with my tonsils till they tingle
tug of war with my tongue
it will grapple with my Adam's apple
all through the day and all night long

There's a frog in my throat . . . it's no joke
There's a frog in my throat . . . it's making me croak
There's a frog in my throat . . . I'm starting to choke
That vicious frog inside my throat is making me a physical wreck
That vicious frog is just a PAIN — IN — THE — NECK!

Bonkers for Conkers

I'm bonkers for conkers
I have a sixty one-er
then Billy's belter battered it
and now it's a gonner.

When creepy crawlies creep and crawl

There are spiders in my wellies
earwigs in my shoe
woodlice in my football boots
I don't know what to do.

Moths have eaten holes
in my favourite pair of socks
ladybirds are on my face
and look like chicken pox.

My jeans are moving by themselves
covered in red ants
and I hate to think what's wriggling
inside my underpants.

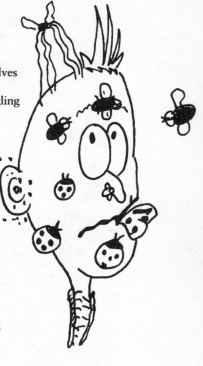

Caterpillars creep around
and nibble on my vest
then weave their cocoons
in the hairs upon my chest.

Stick insects all cling to me
like veins around my throat
bumble bees and wasps
fill the pockets of my coat.

Flies are round my eyes
fleas are in my ear
butterflies flutter by
my mouth then disappear.

There are lots of daddy long legs
like a wig upon my head
beetles in my mittens
and bugs inside my bed.

Slugs, snails, greasy worms
and lots of centipedes
nestle in my armpits
and creep around my sleeves.

There are greenflies up my nostrils
but the funny thing with those
is that they were not green
when they first went up my nose.

When creepy crawlies creep and crawl
busy buzzing side to side.
When creepy crawlies creep and crawl
slither scamper slip and slide.
When creepy crawlies creep and crawl
looking for somewhere to hide
instead of anti-perspirant I wear insecticide.
Every morning every evening
I spray it on from head to toes
in my armpits, down my trousers,
in my ears and up my nose.
Everywhere those creepies crawl
I point my can and spray . . . TTSCHHH!
and then those creepy crawlies
just creep and crawl . . . away.

9

The spearmint spuggy from space stuck on every seat in school

Spuggy on the seat
Chewy on the chair
Bubble gum gunge gets everywhere

It stands on my hands
strands expand like rubber bands.

Congeals and feels like stretch and seal
a scaly skin that you just can't peel.

It smears here inside my ears
and round my eyes . . . bubble gum tears.

Beware! It's there
tangled dread locks in my hair.

Look! It's stuck . . .
a pink punk starfish standing up.

It grows all over my nose
so when I breathe a bubble blows

Like polythene or Plasticine
and the bubble that blows is pink and green.

It's pale, a putrid trail
left by a rubber mutant snail
a string vest made from the blubber from a whale
a slimy slug with a six foot tail
syrup stuck on my fingernails.

SNAP!

It clings like strings
of mouldy maggots and horrible things
on the end of my fingers
a big pink wriggly worm it lingers
so that you cannot distinguish
which is the gum and which are my fingers.

Splashes, splodges, blobs and blots,
blatant blotches, suspect spots,
dabs and dawbs and polka dots
multiplying lots and lots
sticky and strong it has got
the look and feel of alien snot!

Bleargh! Attishyoo!
This alien is trying to kiss you
it's getting to be an issue
one where you wish you
had more than just one Kleenex tissue.

Help! It's drastic
squeezed by snakes of pliable plastic
or an octopus with legs of elastic

Smudges on my shirt
stains on my shoe
a spider's web that's made of glue
I just don't know what to do
with this sticky icky gunged up goo
that pulls so tight my skin turns white
then a nasty ghastly shade of blue.
It's true, I haven't got a clue,
what are we going to do?
It's coming for me and it's coming for you . . .

Invasion of the body snatchers
spuggy on the seats at school will catch us,
plait, matt, attack, attach us.

It's alive and writhes
chokes your throat and blinds your eyes.

Sticks . . . like sick
thick as an oily slick.

Exploding like a can of worms
that slither and slide and slime and squirm.

Spuggy on the seat
Chewy on the chair
Bubble gum gunge gets everywhere.

So beware! It's here and there!
Bubble gum gunge gets everywhere
and I don't know what to do
it's coming for me and it's coming for you
   it's coming for me and it's coming for you
     Be careful what you chew
       Be careful what you chew
         it may just get revenge on you
           so be careful
             what
               you
                 chew

Barry and Beryl the bubble gum blowers

Barry and Beryl the bubble gum blowers
blew bubble gum bubbles as big as balloons.
All shapes and sizes, zebras and zeppelins,
swordfish and sealions, sharks and baboons.
Babies and buckets, bottles and biplanes,
buffaloes, bees, trombones and bassoons.
Yes Barry and Beryl the bubble gum blowers
blew bubble gum bubbles as big as balloons.

Barry and Beryl the bubble gum blowers
blew bubble gum bubbles all over the place.
Big ones in bed, on backseats of buses,
blowing their bubbles in baths with bad taste.
They blew and they bubbled from breakfast till bedtime
the biggest gum bubble that history traced.
One last big breath and the bubble exploded
bursting and blasting their heads into space.
Yes Barry and Beryl the bubble gum blowers
blew bubbles that blasted their heads into space.

Sing that joke

It's always the same:
I'm visiting a primary school,
I've done the performance
It's now lunchtime . . .
And I'm looking for the gents' loo,
Somewhere behind the caretaker's office,
Past the store room and the second on the left
When a small child looks up and says:

"Ey Mister, you're funny you.
  Your're that funny man that came in our assembly.
  You are!
  You're the man who said those daft things.
  You're the man who made us laugh . . .
  Especially when you said rude words in front of the teachers
  That was good that was.
  You made us all join in dead loud . . .
  Even the teachers had to join in
  Can I have your autograph?
  How can you speak so fast?
  Where did you learn to be funny?
  Stacey Hempshall fancies you!
  Do you know my brother? He thinks you're ace.
  Ey Mister, will you sing us that joke again?
  Tell us it again – oh go on!
  Sing us that joke again
  You know the one – where you said "snog"
  Sing us that joke again funny man
  Go on poet man
  Sing us that joke again Mister
  Sing that joke!"

There you have it,
I don't write poems then, they're jokes
And I don't recite them, I sing them.
That's how kids see it so it's fine by me.

Sing that joke again Mister!
Songs and jokes always sound more interesting than poems anyway
So I'm happy to be the funny poet man
Singer of jokes
Especially ones that use words like
Bum, snog, underpants and knickers.

Picnic time on the M25

Picnic time go for a ride
set your sights on the countryside
pack the car and start to drive
stop by the side stop by the side
stop by the side of the M25

Deck chairs on the grass verge
Watch the traffic pass NEEOWN!
Try and pour your flask
Ooh ah ooh ooh eeh
Boiling coffee on your knee

Picnic time go for a ride
set your sights on the countryside
pack the car and start to drive
stop by the side stop by the side
stop by the side of the M25

Salmon spread wholemeal bread
Try to eat as you move your head
Left to right try to bite
Ooh ah ooh ooh eeh
Margarine smeared on your knee

Picnic time go for a ride
set your sights on the countryside
pack the car and start to drive
stop by the side stop by the side
stop by the side of the M25

Picnic time on the M25
Toxic gases will collide
Carbon dioxide
Breathe in SNIFF!
Breathe in SNIFF!
Petrol fumes and lead oxide
Cough splutter cough choke
Poisoned lungs are no joke
Ooh ah ooh ooh eeh
Plan your picnics carefully
Seaside side or countryside
But don't go down to the M25
Don't go down to the M25
Don't — pic — nic — on — the — M — Twenty — Five!

15

Revenge of the hamster

No-one realised, nobody knew
the hamster was sleeping inside my dad's shoe.

He put in his foot and squashed flat its nose
so it opened its jaws and chomped on his toes.

While howling and yowling and hopping like mad
the hamster reeked further revenge on my dad.

It scampered and scurried up his trouser leg
and this time bit something much softer instead.

His eyes bulged and popped like marbles on stalks
and watered while walking the strangest of walks.

16

His ears wiggled wildly while shooting out steam.
All the dogs in the town heard his falsetto scream.

His face went deep purple, his hair stood on end,
his mouth like a letterbox caught in the wind.

The hamster's revenge was almost complete . . .
Dad couldn't sit down for seventeen weeks.

Now dad doesn't give the hamster a chance . . .
He wears stainless steel socks and hamster proof pants.

God made the elephant timeless

God made the elephant royal
with regal swaying motion
rippling skin like shifting seas
eternal as the ocean.

God made the elephant graceful
an animal at peace
mighty yet so gentle
the king and queen of beasts.

God made the elephant beautiful
a life to be enjoyed.
Man saw only money
so this beauty was destroyed.

God made the elephant timeless
past, present and beyond
but with each creature slaughtered
that time is almost gone.

Catch of the day's shoal of the season

Always choose an octopus for goalie
Always have a whale for the defensive wall
Always have a salmon for high crosses
Never let a swordfish head the ball at all.

Never make an enemy of a sea anenoma
Never have a clash with a giant clam
Never pull a muscle in a tackle or a tussle
Always let the kipper be the skipper if you can.

Always have a mackerel to tackle well
Always have a stingray staying in the wing
Always have a shark — he's an expert at attack
Never kiss a jellyfish who scores with a sting.

There are eels who feel electric playing at a pace that's hectic
and the lobster's going potty scoring from an indirect kick.
There are dolphins doing dribbling weaving round shoals,
helping whelks, out thinking winkles, getting lots of goals.

Mediterranean, Pacific and Atlantic
the football is specific yet very very frantic.
Million of matches of varying degrees
in the twenty thousand leagues under the seas.

Bullies and their messengers

Have you noticed how bullies always have gangs
and never ever walk alone.
They never speak to you one to one,
it's always some little messenger
who comes up to you and says
'Watchityordedcosmybigmate'sgonnagetyouRIGHT!'

Bullies messengers are always small.
Always.
By themselves they're nothing, nobodies,
who hide in shadows on the way home,
never saying boo to a goose
. . . but when they're with their big mates
they think they're big hard tough guy fighters
who say big hard tough guy things like
'IfyoutouchmeI'llgetmybigmateontoyouSOWATCHIT!'

Bullies and their messengers
are always always small people inside
hiding in large groups,
pretending that they're really tough
when really they are frightened nobodies
scared to be alone,
and if by chance you do catch them alone
they will be just as scared as you might be
and they will be just as likely to walk away silently
as they are to start a fight with you
because bullies and their messengers are cowards
yes, bullies and their messengers are cowards
and that, my friends, is very very true.

All I want is a friend

All I want is a friend she said.
All I want is a friend.

To sit with me in class.
To talk about last night's telly with.

A friend to have dinner with.
A friend to stand in the playground with.

All I want is a friend she said
as she sat silently down
next to someone who didn't really like her
next to someone who just ignored her
next to someone who made faces at her
and talked about her behind her back.

First kisses

First kisses are worrying.
I mean, what do you do?
And is there a right way of doing it?

Do you keep your lips closed tight
and rub them side to side?

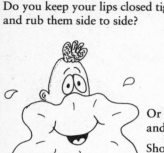

Or do you leave them open
and let them go all squishy and wobbly?

Should you do sink plunger impressions?

Do you close your eyes,
or is it safer to leave them open
— at least until you know
that you're not going to bang noses?

What happens if both your glasses
steam up at the same time?

Or your braces get caught on theirs?

What if their wobbly tooth comes out?
What about if you dribble?

ATCHOO!

Be careful if you sneeze . . . you might blow their head off!

And what do you do if you breathe in suddenly?

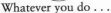

Whatever you do . . .
And whoever you do it with . . .
Just remember this one very very important rule:
Make sure that the first person you ever ever kiss
does not have a runny nose.

Infants and assemblies: the school nose picking champion

He's really easy to pick out.
About five rows back, it looks like
a snail has crawled out of each nostril,
wound its way across his face . . . then hidden in his ears.

The trail has then dried and gone all crusty,
like a green three dimensional handlebar moustache
and he's looking for the school's biggest bogey.
Very often from up his best friend's nose.

Collecting bits off all his friends
he moulds and moulds
and somtimes moulds and chews . . .

Have you ever met a Yeti with a taste for spaghetti?

Have you ever met a Yeti with a taste for spaghetti?
Or a bison with his eyes on the currant buns with ice on?
A sharp fanged shark with a taste for treacle tart?
Or a pig in a wig that's pink and big?

Have you ever met a bee who liked honey in his tea?
Or a lion with a tie on at a table with a pie on?
A butterfly flutter by in trousers with a cut off thigh?
Or a cycling pike on a mountain bike?

Have you ever met a llama with a liking for banana?
Or a small short sighted snail supping strong and real ale?
A tame and ten ton tiger drinking twenty pints of Tizer?
Or a sheep counting people trying to sleep?

Have you ever seen a stork savour sweet and sour pork?
A resourceful horse with a course of radish sauce?
Milkshake making from a cow a snake is shaking?
Or a cricket mad bat in pads and hat?

Did you ever see a chicken that liked human finger licking?
Or a crocodile rock a while smiling with a lot of style?
A pelican whose bill it can eat more than its belly can?
Or a multicoloured punk mohican skunk?

Have you ever seen these creatures
with strange habits and odd features?
No?
Neither have I.

It's not the same anymore

It's not the same since Patch died.
Sticks are just sticks.
Never thrown, never fetched.

It's not the same anymore.
Tennis balls lie still and lifeless.
The urge to bounce them has gone.

It's not the same now.
I can't bring myself to whistle.
There's no reason to do so.

His collor hangs on the hook
and his name tag and lead are dusty.

His basket and bowl are in a plastic bag
lying at an angle on a garage shelf.

My new slippers will never be chewed
and I've no excuse for my lack of homework anymore.

I can now watch the football in peace, uninterrupted.
No frantic barking and leaping just when it gets to the goal.

I don't have to share my sweets and biscuits
and then wipe the dribbling drool off my trouser legs.

It's just not the same anymore.
When Patch died a small part of me died too.

All that's left is a mound of earth
and my hand made cross beneath the apple tree.

All that's left are the memories.
Thousands of them.

It's just not the same anymore.

These are the hands that wave
These are the hands that clap
These are the hands that pray
These are the hands that slap

These are the hands that grip
These are the hands that write
These are the hands that point
These are the hands that fight

These are the hands that hold
These are the hands that love
These are the hands of mine
That fit me like a glove.

I never cried when my Grandma died
You see I was away from home at the time
The first time I saw my Grandfather afterwards
he was watching World Cup Football on the telly.
He told me that it was a good match and that
the goalie had made some fantastic saves
although we were still one nil down.
But somewhere behind his eyes
a light had dimmed
and on the other side of his glasses
I could see teardrops forming
and as they fell down his face
they weren't because
his team had lost
but because he had lost
his team.

You see, to my Grandfather
my Grandmother was his best team
in the world.
Ever.

The colours in God's paint box

If I wasn't me
I'd like to be a colour from God's paint box.

Maybe a green that would shade
a thousand different leaves
on a thousand different trees
the green that causes emeralds to shine
the glint in a kitten's eyes
the liquid freshness of the ocean
or the lush moistness of the rainforest.

Possibly a blue
whether the pastel peaceful sky
the splash on the wing of a Jay
the deep sea calmness
the paleness of a Blackbird's eggshell
or the electric flash of storms.

The red slash of poppy fields
the thickened shades of blood
the crimson sheen of appleskin
the petals on a rosebush
or the setting sun at eventide.

A million shades of blue
and a million shades of green.
A million shades of every hue
and a million inbetween.
Colours clash then melt together
in God's Royal Flush
and drip in perfect shades
from His one and only brush.

A quick glance through my photo album

Snapshots may capture one single moment in time
but looking at them now
these images bleed animated real life
as every door is opened
and the stories flow in detail once again.

Dad falling into the pond head first
while trying to rescue Rex the cat from the tree.

Sister's dayglo orange perm gone wrong,
brother's green mohican and nose ring,
mum and dad's embarrassment
at our posh cousin's wedding.

The day we won the cup
and mum got told off by the police
for dancing on the pitch.

The school trip to Scafell Pike where on the group photo
everyone smiles and pulls tongues
except boring Mr. Goodwood who doesn't like children
and Wrighty . . . who later got done for mooning.

Posing with my first guitar,
all sunglasses, sneer and spots
in front of my Slade and Mud posters,
not knowing the guitar was upside down.

And that one, the small one,
all blurred and squashed from the booth at Woollies.
That's me and Sally, my first real girlfriend,
smiling and eating Curly Wurlies.
(It's a good job that was the last photo of the four,
ten seconds later and the camera would have caught us
in the middle of a slurpy chocolate snog . . .)

Good times.
Good times indeed . . .

The magic kitchen carpet

There's an old and tattered carpet
on the kitchen floor,
weatherbeaten, motheaten,
just behind the door.

Foodstained, colour drained,
it's shabby and it's torn.
Dead bare, threadbare,
weathered and it's worn.

On this tattered magic carpet
you can choose your destination.
Any wild adventure.
Any situation.

When the cooking's hot and bubbling
we're somewhere hot and tropical.
When wearing Grandma's glasses
we're somewhere microscopical.

When the ironing is steaming
we're deep in the Sahara,
Red Indians on the warpath
with mum's lipstick and mascara.

When the washer overflows
we're in shark infested seas.
When the freezer door is open
we are in an Arctic breeze.

We are rockets high in space
when mum does the hoovering.
When she's moving chairs and tables
we're like warplanes out manouevering.

Assorted jars and bottles means
experiments and science.
When dad leaves his wellies there
we're in the land of giants.

With pebbles from those welly treads
there's caverns full of rubble
but if he drags the mud in
then we all get into trouble!

There's a magic kitchen carpet
just behind the door
weatherbeaten, motheaten,
covering the floor.

On this tattered magic carpet
you can choose your destination
because nothing's quite as magical
as your imagination.

This year I will stay awake

This year I will stay awake
all night long make no mistake.
On this Christmas Eve I'll keep
my eyes open, try to peep.
This year I won't drowse or dream
but be alert till Santa's been,
see just what he leaves and how
he fits down our chimney now,
how the presents all appear
hear the sleighbells and reindeeer.
This year I will not count sheep
but pretend to be asleep.
No catnaps or forty winks
or dropping off with slower blinks.
This year there will be no slumber
I won't let myself go under.
This year I won't nod or doze.
or let my heavy eyelids close.
This year I won't nod or doze
or let my heavy eyelids close
or let my heavy eyelids close
or let my he . . avy eye . . li . . ds clo . . se
or let my he . . avy eye . . liiids clo . . zzzzzzzzzzzzzzzzzzzzzzzzzzzzz

The day after the day after Boxing Day

On the day after the day after Boxing Day
Santa wakes, up eventually,
puts away his big red suit and wellies,
lets Rudolph and the gang out into the meadow
then shaves his head and beard.

He puts on his new cool sunglasses,
baggy blue Bermuda shorts (he's sick of red),
yellow stripey T shirt that doesn't quite cover his belly
and lets his toes breathe in flip flops.

Packing a bucket and spade,
fifteen tubes of Factor Twenty suncream
and seventeen romantic novels
he fills his Walkman with the latest sounds,
is glad to use a proper suitcase instead of the old sack
and heads off into the Mediterranean Sunrise
enjoying the comforts of a Boeing 747
(although he passes on the free drinks).

Six months later,
relaxed, red and a little more than stubbly,
he looks at his watch, adjusts his wide brimmed sun hat,
mops the sweat from his brow and strokes his chin
wondering why holidays always seem to go so quickly.

Anthony's birthday

Anthony had a birthday
but everyone had forgotten.
In fact not only had they forgotten
but they had been invited to another party.
He saw them all going
in their party hats and party clothes
with big smiles and big presents
and he sat there
uninvited.
Silent.
By himself.
Anthony felt lonely.
On his special day he felt left out.
Rejected.
And he cried
and imagined how Jesus may feel
on the 25th of December.
Every year.

Stables

Stables are unhealthy places,
not somewhere you are likely to invite a friend or posh company
for a quiet chat and a cup of tea.

Stables are dirty places,
containing vast amounts of straw,
covering vast amounts of dung and droppings
which doesn't smell that good really.

Stables are places you would expect to find animals inhabiting.
Animals such as horses, donkeys, cows, sheep, geese, hens,
ducks, rats, mice, fleas, spiders, lice and lots of other messy things.

Stables are not quiet places,
but places of whinnying, braying, mooing,
bleating, cackling, clucking, quacking,
squeaking, scratching, buzzing and general confusion.

All in all, stables are pretty unhealthy places,
not really somewhere you would expect a child to be born,
never mind a King.

I'd rather draw nil nil

I can't be doing with all this hugging
and kissing and falling over
and cuddling for five minutes
every time I score a goal.

I'd rather draw nil nil.

Unless Jayne's playing . . . in which case it's different.

Then I'd rather win six nil
and score a double hat trick.

Infants and assemblies: sitting still and speech patterns

Bottom shufflers
Head wobblers
Arm stretchers
They lean forward and . . .

Stroke your trousers
Play tiggy with your shoes
Pull the hairs on your legs
Put Sooty puppets up the inside of your trouser legs.

Assembly Halls regulate speech patterns
All over the country children talk in exactly the same way.
It doesn't matter about regional accents . . .
North, south, east, west. they all say
"Gerr – rrd Mmmoooorrr – ninnnng Ev – reee – bod – deeeee!"

Drinking the dregs from the staffroom cups

Griff and me had a dare.
Who would be brave enough to . . .
drink all the dregs from the teacher's cups in the staffroom.

We stayed late last night,
waited till all the teachers had gone home
then crept into the staffroom.
What a mess! Paper, books, half eaten sandwiches . . .
apple cores, yoghurt pots, banana skins, crisp crumbs . . .
chocolate wrappers, mouldy milk . . .
and our homework from last year.
Blimey! It was worse than my little brother's bedroom.

We collected all the cups onto one table.
Thirty seven of them all together.
Some were more than half full.
All were cold and slimy with skin on the top.
Most were green and furry . . . different shades of green.
It looked like a science experiment.
I thought the green was mould.
Griff thought it was alien slime from Mr. Hooter's nose.
Several cups had cigarette ends in.
Others had floaty white lumps
which could have been congealed powdered milk, cheese
or chalkdust . . . or possibly all three.
At least one seemed to have been soup
judging by the unidentifiable blobs encrusted round the rim.
I thought I could see some croutons or breadcrumbs in there
somewhere but Griff though differently . . .
He said the flakey bits were old Mr. Raymond's dandruff.

Anyway, the dare was . . .
to drink as many as possible without stopping.
We looked at each other, held our noses, took a deep breath
— then had a much better idea
and emptied all the dregs in the teacher's tea-pot,
the big brown one that's always there.
We mixed them all up with a big stick,
added a bit of washing up liquid, a slice of school gravy,
several chewed up fingernails, a tube of my spot cream,
a quick spray of Ralgex, four dead flys from the sink,
my used tissue and one of Griff's football socks
then put the top back on.

Today, outside the staffroom,
we heard the teachers talking as they ran to the toilets.
They said how clean their cups were for a change
and how the tea tasted much nicer than usual.

41

Teacher's very quiet today

Teacher's very quiet today,
hasn't shouted once
but just let us get on with things
in a casual sort of way.

Several times I caught her gaze
but I wasn't even noticed.
Teacher looks preoccupied
like something's weighing heavy on her mind.

I don't know what it is
but I think I've seen that look before.
The expression seems familiar
but not in school.

It's more like the look dad had
when he crashed his new car
or mum when she found out
Auntie Jo was ill.

Teacher's very quiet today,
hasn't shouted once
but just let us get on with things
in a casual sort of way.

Mathematically telepathically magical

Think of a number from one to ten.
Any one will do.
Are you ready with your number then . . .
multiply it by two.

Once you have the answer
add another six.
Have you got this total?
Here's what you do next . . .

Halve the total you have got
(and this is the magical mystery)
Subtract the number you first thought of
and your answer must be . . . three!

It's mathematically telepathically magical you see.
It works with any number from one right up to ten.
Carefully follow each of the steps, your answer's always three.
Think of another number and try it again and again.

The school trip to the art gallery and museum

We had to be quiet, dead quiet.
Dead sometimes being the operative word.

We weren't allowed to eat crisps and drink pop,
cough, sneeze or hiccup
in case we disturbed the peaceful ambient atmosphere —
The dead silence.

We weren't allowed to walk at our own pace
and look at what we wanted but had to spend equal time
gazing at chandeliers and table legs.

We weren't allowed to yawn while the droning guide
went on for hours about the historical significance
of the painting and how it captured perfectly
a moment in history with its original oil on canvas technique and
individually carved gold leaf mahogany frames
that took fifteen years to complete, another two to mount
and fifteen seconds to look at.

We weren't allowed to ask questions like
'Does the gift shop sell sweets?'

And we definitely weren't allowed to laugh out loud
at the fat bottomed Victorian nude bathing ladies
and point at the little rude bits on the Greek style statue
that looked like our Headmaster.

So, we saw . . .
Sunflowers and sunsets, poppies and portraits,
stickmen and smog, splodges and splashes,
various vases and pieces of pottery . . .

But the best bits were . . .
the mummies in bandages
the skulls and the skeletons
dinosaur bones, stuffed eagles and bears,
Viking helmets, swords and spears and sharp pointy things
with hooks on the end that could easily pop a man's eye out.

Yes, the best bits were
laughing at the fat wobbly bottoms on the nude bathing ladies
and pointing at the little rude bits on the Greek statue
that looked just like our Headmaster.

Yes, that was great
but the really best bits were when my mate Oddy
popped his crisp bag really loud and woke up three old ladies
and an attendant then got caught putting the Headmaster's name
on a sign next to the Greek statue.

And it was dead brill when we were allowed
to spend our pocket money in the gift shop and we all bought
sweets, a pencil sharpener and key ring
with the name of the gallery on in gold
and everyone — and I mean everyone (even the other teachers)
bought a postcard of the Greek statue
that looked like our Headmaster.

Things were different then

Dad always says
When I was young, well things were different then.

Games were games. Proper games.
We used to have to make our own entertainment.
Not all this whizz bang flash computer stuff
with blood and guts and gore.
No zapping and violence and all that.
We used to play cowboys and Indians, or hide and seek.

Music was real music as well.
Songs with real words and catchy tunes
played by musicians, proper musicians,
. . . Elvis, The Beatles, The Rolling Stones,
instead of people who can't sing pushing a keyboard programme
to make a repetitive headache inducing beat
while they jump up and down like lunatics
shouting a meaningless phrase over and over again.

And footballers . . . huh!
All this kissing and cuddling!
All this rolling round on the floor!
All this diving and cheating!
All this crying when they don't win!
They spend more time on their hairstyles
than they do on their skills, more like a woman's game,
not like Bobby Charlton, Geoff Hurst or Jimmy Greaves.
Real players they were.

Looking through Gran's old scrapbook
of photos and cuttings
I found my dad
dressed up as a sherriff
water pistol and spud gun
aimed at the dog's head.

There was a newspaper clipping of him at a talent contest
with a plastic guitar mouthing the words to a song
the newspaper quoted him as singing
'Do wah diddy diddy dum diddy do'
or something like that.

DO WAH KIDDY!

Then there was his school football team photo
where everyone looked like girls, hippies or both
and the teacher had a Kevin Keegan perm.

My dad says things were different then
but they weren't really.

I Wish I'd Been present at Christmas past

I wish I'd been a shepherd
and heard the angels sing.
I wish I'd been to Bethlehem
and seen the Infant King.

I wish I'd been a wise man
at the stable bare
following the star with
gold, frankincense and myrhh.

I wish I'd been an animal
who shared my manger hay
with that special new born baby
on that first Christmas Day.

The magic, the meaning, the reason and the season

Lose the magic lose the meaning
Lose the meaning lose the reason
Lose the reason lose the magic
Lose the magic lose the season.

Jesus and Santa

I reckon Jesus and Santa would get on well.
Really well.
I bet they could be best friends.
I mean they've got loads in common . . .

Everybody likes them at Christmas
and sings lots of songs about them.

Everybody tells their children about the magic
of presents, stars, shepherds, chimneys and red nosed reindeer.

Everybody tries to be nice to each other
and make an extra effort because of them.

People even think of others less well off
and give a little more to charity.

All because of the Christmas spirit.
All because of Father Christmas and Jesus.

Everybody thinks of them on that one special day
when Jesus was born and Father Christmas leaves his gifts.

Nobody thinks about the hard work
and all the good things they do for the rest of the year.

Anoraks at feeding time

My baby brother loves his food.
He loves it when it is between his fingers.
He loves it when it is in his hair.
He loves it when it is in his ears.
He loves it when it is up his nose.
He loves it when it is down his shirt.
And sometimes he loves it when it is in his mouth.

Most of all he loves it when it is in his mouth
and he can blow a great big raspeberry
and spray it all over mum and dad.
Sometimes, at the exact moment
that they put the spoon near his mouth
he sneezes . . . ATCHOOOO!
and the food goes everywhere . . .
up the walls and down his high chair
on the ceiling and across the room
right between the dog's eyes
all over the budgie
in mummy's hair
in daddy's ears
up mummy's nose
down daddy's shirt.

He thinks that it is a great game
and laughs and giggles at all the mess.

My baby brother loves his food.
Mum and dad now wear anoraks at feeding time.

Revenge of the fly

One day while eating breakfast,
bacon, ham and eggs,
a little fly buzzed down upon
the top of Billy's head.
Its little furry feet tickled
across young Billy's brow
and then it flew away
and he thought "It's okay now."
He cut a piece of bacon,
looking forward to its taste,
was just about to munch it up
and then, across his face
he felt a little tickle
as the fly came in to land . . .
the bacon was uneaten
as the fork fell from his hand.
He shook his head and waved his arms
up, down and side to side
but the little fly just held on tight
no matter what he tried.
Just then the little fly buzzed off
and Billy with an evil grin said

51

He found a rolled up newspaper,
a tea towel and a shoe.
He lay in wait, his breakfast – bait
and knew what he would do.
He heard a little buzzing noise
and then he heard it stop.
Creeping out then with a shout
he let the towel drop.
Armed with the shoe and paper
he laughed above the plate,
the fly beneath the towel
would not, could not escape.
He brought the paper flying down
with a squelchy soggy SPLAT!
With an evil laugh he said
"Take that! And that! And that!"
The show crashed down until the plate
was smashed to smithereens
and a sticky, lumpy, splodgy mess
was all that could be seen.
Billy heard no buzzing now
but he heard his mum come in
so picking up the evidence
he threw it in the bin.

But, that night as Billy slept,
his window open wide
ten thousand million million flies
buzzed silently inside . . .
they hovered in the deadly swarm
above young Billy's bed
and with a shout of "Tally Ho!"
they flew right at his head!
Up his nose, inside his ears,
across his sleeping eyes,
on his tongue and down his throat
they blocked up his insides.
No-one heard him shout.
No-one heard him cry
so just remember that
next time you kill a fly.
And if, by chance, you do kill one
then when you go to bed
make sure you close all windows
and cover up your head . . .

Four Crazy Pets

I've four crazy pets, all rather jolly –
Rover, Tiddles, Flopsy and Polly.
A dog, a rabbit, a parrot and a cat.
Which one's which? Can you guess that?

Rover's a dog? No!
Tiddles is a cat? No!
Flopsy's a rabbit? No!
Polly's a parrot? No!

My dog has the appetite of a small gorilla.
We called her Polly 'cause we can never fill her.

The rabbit has a habit of wetting where we're standing.
We call him Tiddles 'cause the puddles keep expanding.

Our cat purrs like an engine turning over.
Vroom vroom vroom – so we call her Rover.

The fact that our parrot cannot fly is such a shame.
Flopsy by nature and Flopsy by name.

Four crazy names! Wouldn't you agree?
I think my pets fit their names purrfectly.

The greatest storyteller ever

Jesus must have told the greatest stories,
the funniest jokes and known all the best tricks.

If he didn't
no way would any of the children
want to spend any length of time with him.

And the disciples actually had to turn them away
so Jesus must have told the greatest stories,
the funniest jokes and known all the best tricks.
Ever.

Wrigglebum John

Wrigglebum John
Wrigglebum John
He's got a chair that he won't sit on.

Fidget left
Fidget right
Fidget through the day and night.

Wrigglebum John
Wrigglebum John
He's got a chair that he won't sit on.

Every day,
Hour and minute
He's got a chair but he can't stay in it.

On the tables watch him crawl
Climbing up and down the wall
Swinging from the lights and curtains
Of one thing you can be certain
Jumping, running, skipping, hopping
You have not a chance of stopping

Wrigglebum John
Wrigglebum John
He's got a chair that he won't sit on.

Now he's here, now he's gone.
He doesn't stay around for long.
Where does he get his energy from?
Wrigglebum Wrigglebum Wrigglebum John
Wrigglebum Wrigglebum Wrigglebum John
Wrigglebum Wrigglebum Wrigglebum . . . JOHN!

Real poetry does not use the word 'bum'

I could tell straightaway that the Headmistress didn't like me.
There I was in her school
— in front of her pupils
all three hundred and fifty of them.
Me, the visiting 'poet and writer',
and I could tell straightaway that she didn't like me.
It was the way she sat,
side on, never looking me full in the face
but sneering and wrinkling her nose
while her pupils,
all three hundred and fifty of them,
laughed at the jokes in the funny poems,
joined in noisily in the loud poems
and listened quietly to the thoughtful ones.

Even at the end of the hour
with the pupils,
all three hundred and fifty of them
bright eyed and clapping,
she still didn't like me
and while the pupils,
not quite all three hundred and fifty of them,
asked for autographs, remembering lines
and telling me their favourite bits
she hovered in the distance
side on, never looking me full in the face
and I could tell that all the time she was thinking
'Real poetry does not use the word "bum" . . .'

And I looked at the other teachers
leading laughing children back to classrooms
smiling and repeating choruses together
and knew that not one of them would agree with her at all.

Let no one steal your dreams

Let no-one steal your dreams
Let no-one tear apart
That burning of ambition
That fires the drive inside your heart.

Let no-one steal your dreams
Let no-one tell you that you can't
Let no-one hold you back
Let no-one tell you that you won't.

Set your sights and keep them fixed
Set your sights on high
Let no-one steal your dreams
Your only limit is the sky.

Let no-one steal those dreams
Follow your heart
Follow your soul
For only when you follow them
Will you feel truly whole.

Set your sights and keep them fixed
Set your sights on high
Let no-one steal your dreams
Your only limit is the sky.